ideals

THANKSGIVING

Autumn calls to harvesttime
When gold and yellow fruits of field
And garden plot reflect the love
Of God amid her lavish yield.

Autumn calls each thankful heart
To kneel in thankful prayer and praise,
And sing a psalm of gratitude
For life's happy thanksgiving days.

Harold A. Schulz

Editorial Director, James Kuse
Managing Editor, Ralph Luedtke
Associate Editor, Colleen Callahan Gonring
Production Editor/Manager, Richard Lawson
Photographic Editor, Gerald Koser
Copy Editor, Sharon Style

Thanksgiving Prayer

O come, let us sing unto the Lord:
Let us heartily rejoice in the strength of our salvation.
Let us come before his presence with thanksgiving.
And show ourselves glad in him with psalms.

For the Lord is a great God,
And a great King above all gods.
In his hands are all the corners of the earth:
The strength of the hills is his also.

The sea is his, and he made it:
And his hands prepared the dry land.
O come, let us worship and bow down:
Let us kneel before the Lord our maker.

For he is the Lord our God:
And we are the people of his pasture
And the sheep of his hand.

Psalm 95

ISBN 0-89542-327-8 295

IDEALS—Vol. 36 No. 7 October MCMLXXIX, IDEALS (ISSN 0019-137X) is published eight times a year,
January, February, April, June, July, September, October, November
by IDEALS PUBLISHING CORPORATION, 11315 Watertown Plank Road, Milwaukee, Wis. 53226
Second class postage paid at Milwaukee, Wisconsin. Copyright © MCMLXXIX by IDEALS PUBLISHING CORPORATION.
Postmaster, please send form 3579 to Ideals Publishing Corporation, 175 Community Drive, Great Neck, New York, 11025
All rights reserved. Title IDEALS registered U.S. Patent Office.
Published Simultaneously in Canada

ONE YEAR SUBSCRIPTION—eight consecutive issues as published—only $15.95
TWO YEAR SUBSCRIPTION—sixteen consecutive issues as published—only $27.95
SINGLE ISSUES—only $2.95

A Thanksgiving Prayer

Reginald Holmes

We pause this day
And offer thanks to Him
Who has bestowed with loving hand
The fruitful bounties of the land,
A cup filled to the brim;
And thus we pray:

That Thou provide
Our needs for future days;
Clear blue skies and sunny weather
For men to dwell in peace together;
And as we sing Thy praise,
Walk by our side.

Teach us the way
To know and do Thy will.
Help us to share as all men should
While keeping faith and doing good
As we Thy plans fulfill;
For this we pray.

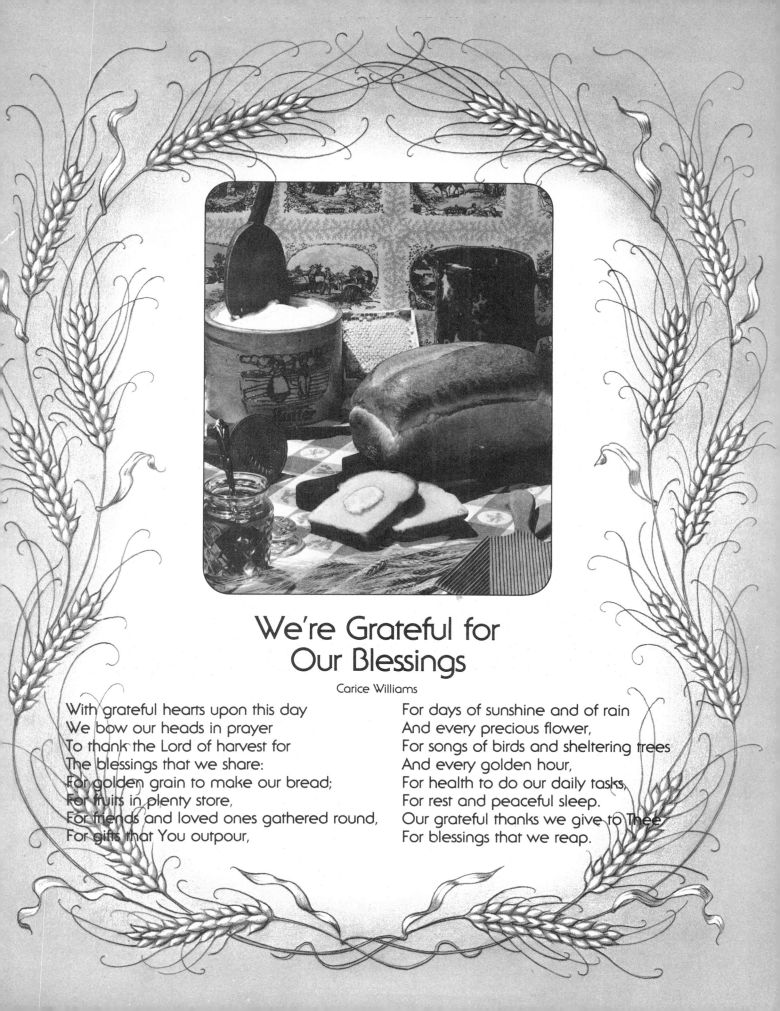

We're Grateful for
Our Blessings

Carice Williams

With grateful hearts upon this day
We bow our heads in prayer
To thank the Lord of harvest for
The blessings that we share:
For golden grain to make our bread;
For fruits in plenty store,
For friends and loved ones gathered round,
For gifts that You outpour,

For days of sunshine and of rain
And every precious flower,
For songs of birds and sheltering trees
And every golden hour,
For health to do our daily tasks,
For rest and peaceful sleep.
Our grateful thanks we give to Thee
For blessings that we reap.

A Prayer at Thanksgiving

Dear Lord, as autumn drops across the land,
A crisp reminder of chill days ahead,
The sight of falling leaves on every hand,
And hillsides etched in sparkling gold and red—

We ask thy guidance for the family here.
Our work, receive all blessings from above,
That we may have a most successful year,
Give us your grace and ever constant love—

Keep us forever in a watchful glow
And may we never fail to do thy will;
So looking down upon us here below
Our hearts with all your heavenly peace fulfill—

This is our prayer, that we may spread the light
Of truth to all who labor in thy sight.

Marian L. Moore

Henry Wadsworth Longfellow

Born in Portland, Maine, in 1807, Henry Wadsworth Longfellow came from a family steeped in American traditions. His ancestors included a general in the American Revolution as well as Pilgrims from Plymouth. This American heritage played an important role in his poetry. Although his father wanted Longfellow to join him in his legal practice, he embarked on a literary career and entered Bowdoin College, where he was influenced by the works of Sir Walter Scott and Washington Irving. Because of his aptitude for foreign languages, upon his graduation from Bowdoin College, he was offered a professorship of modern languages there. He went on to preside over the foreign language department at Harvard. Longfellow combined his foreign language aptitude and poetic ability in a most noteworthy translation of Dante's *Divine Comedy*. Not neglecting his desire to write poetry, he became one of the leading American balladists, writing such romantic legends as *The Song of Hiawatha, The Courtship of Miles Standish, Tales of a Wayside Inn*, and perhaps his most beloved poem, *Evangeline, A Tale of Love in Acadie, Home of the Happy*. Shortly after his death in 1882 a memorial to Longfellow was unveiled in Westminster Abbey. In 1900 he was elected to the American Hall of Fame. Longfellow acquired a sense of patience and strength which was echoed in the gentleness of his poetry and imparted through romantic legend. Longfellow remains one of America's most beloved balladists.

Autumn

With what a glory comes and goes the year!
The buds of spring, those beautiful harbingers
Of sunny skies and cloudless times, enjoy
Life's newness, and earth's garniture spread out;
And when the silver habit of the clouds
Comes down upon the autumn sun, and with
A sober gladness the old year takes up
His bright inheritance of golden fruits,
A pomp and pageant fill the splendid scene.

There is a beautiful spirit breathing now
Its mellow richness on the clustered trees,
And, from a beaker full of richest dyes,
Pouring new glory on the autumn woods,
And dipping in warm light the pillared clouds.
Morn on the mountain, like a summer bird,
Lifts up her purple wing, and in the vales
The gentle wind, a sweet and passionate wooer,
Kisses the blushing leaf, and stirs up life
Within the solemn woods of ash deep-crimsoned,

And silver beech, and maple yellow-leaved,
Where Autumn, like a faint old man, sits down
By the wayside aweary. Through the trees
The golden robin moves. The purple finch,
That on wild cherry and red cedar feeds,
A winter bird, comes with its plaintive whistle,
And pecks by the witch hazel, whilst aloud
From cottage roofs the warbling bluebird sings,
And merrily, the oft-repeated stroke,
Sounds from the threshing floor the busy flail.

Oh, what a glory doth this world put on
For him who, with a fervent heart, goes forth
Under the bright and glorious sky, and looks
On duties well performed, and days well spent!
For him the wind, ay, and the yellow leaves,
Shall have a voice, and give him eloquent teachings.
He shall so hear the solemn hymn that death
Has lifted up for all, that he shall go
To his long resting place without a tear.

The Day Is Done

The day is done, and the darkness
Falls from the wings of night,
As a feather is wafted downward
From an eagle in his flight.

I see the lights of the village
Gleam through the rain and the mist,
And a feeling of sadness comes o'er me,
That my soul cannot resist:

A feeling of sadness and longing,
That is not akin to pain,
And resembles sorrow only
As the mist resembles the rain.

Come, read to me some poem,
Some simple and heartfelt lay,
That shall soothe this restless feeling,
And banish the thoughts of day.

Not from the grand old masters,
Not from the bards sublime,
Whose distant footsteps echo
Through the corridors of time.

For, like strains of martial music,
Their mighty thoughts suggest
Life's endless toil and endeavour;
And tonight I long for rest.

Read from some humbler poet,
Whose songs gushed from his heart,
As showers from the clouds of summer,
Or tears from the eyelids start;

Who, through long days of labor,
And nights devoid of ease,
Still heard in his soul the music
Of wonderful melodies.

Such songs have power to quiet
The restless pulse of care,
And come like the benediction
That follows after prayer.

Then read from the treasured volume
The poem of thy choice,
And lend to the rhyme of the poet
The beauty of thy voice.

And the night shall be filled with music,
And the cares that infest the day,
Shall fold their tents, like the Arabs,
And as silently, steal away.

The Rainy Day

The day is cold, and dark, and dreary:
It rains, and the wind is never weary;
The vine still clings to the mouldering wall,
But at every gust the dead leaves fall,
And the day is dark and dreary.

My life is cold, and dark, and dreary;
It rains, and the wind is never weary;
My thoughts still cling to the mouldering past,
But the hopes of youth fall thick in the blast,
And the days are dark and dreary.

Be still, sad heart! and cease repining;
Behind the clouds is the sun still shining;
Thy fate is the common fate of all,
Into each life some rain must fall,
Some days must be dark and dreary.

Autumn

Thou comest, autumn, heralded by the rain,
With banners, by great gales incessant fanned,
Brighter than brightest silks of Samarcand,
And stately oxen harnessed to thy wain!

Thou standest, like imperial Charlemagne,
Upon thy bridge of gold; thy royal hand
Outstretched with benedictions o'er the land,
Blessing the farms through all thy vast domain.

Thy shield is the red harvest moon, suspended
So long beneath the heaven's o'erhanging eaves;
Thy steps are by the farmer's prayers attended;
Like flames upon an altar shine the sheaves;

And, following thee, in thy ovation splendid,
Thine almoner, the wind, scatters the golden leaves!

The Pageantry of Autumn

When Autumn moves with silent step
Across the summer scene,
She weaves a vivid fabric
To cover the woodland green.
Over the quiet countryside,
In glorious array,
Over the field and meadow,
She spreads her bright display.

She weaves with threads of
    brilliant hues
And fashions a tapestry bold
Of rich brown earth and flaming fire
And sunlight's shimmering gold.
Autumn's reign is swift and fleeting;
It is Nature's final fling
Before the quiet, calm repose
The winter months will bring.

Alexa Kirsten

Thankful for this Day

Across the hills, across the land,
A hymn of gratitude and praise
Resounds from every heart and woodland grove,
As we count our blessings,
As we marvel at this autumn day!

Let us know the joy of living . . .
When earth's rich harvest lies before us
A splendor to behold,
When loved ones are around us
And we have a wealth more durable than gold,
When our hearts are filled with gratitude
For blessings untold,
When we can clasp another's hand
And lead him in from the cold.

Let us know the joy of living . . .
When the hills are vibrant and alive,
Clad in a bright array,
When flaming crimson and brilliant gold
Light up a hill's pathway,
When Autumn casts her amber glow
To cheer and brighten our day,
When she sees our summer flowers,
Nipped by the frost, slowly fade away.

Across the hills, across the land,
Let us sing our hymn of praise,
For God hath shed his glorious light
On this most golden of his days!

Joy Belle Burgess

Song of Thanksgiving

Blue mists of Indian summer
Veiling the flaming hills,
As the rhapsody of autumn

Over the countryside spills . . .
Song of the farmer singing,
Song of the season's yield,

Song in his heart of Thanksgiving
Bestowed from vine and field.
Song of our Pilgrim Fathers

For bounties of the land,
Symbolic of God's great blessing
For His children on every hand,

As He pours out the horn of plenty
In abundance across the land.

Angie Davidson Bass

For Fruited Vine

For fruited vine, and shining fields of grain,
    And hearth and home this golden autumn day;
For cimsoned leaf and silvered sheets of rain
    That came, in blessing, as we knelt to pray;

For fair child faces in the lamplight glow
    When work is done, when mists of evening veil
The quiet earth as sunset clouds flame low
    Above the ripened corn and nested quail—

Give thanks to God from whom each good gift came,
    And raise the flag of hope in freedom's name.
Our Pilgrim fathers voiced in grateful prayer
    Thanksgiving for that first glad harvest yield;

And in their small log church gave to His care
    Those pioneers in primal wood and field.
And we— who claim as heritage the soil
    They tilled and consecrated here— are free

To dream and build through steadfast faith and toil
    The bulwark of the race: democracy.
Let us give thanks with love that cannot die
    And raise our star-hung banner to the sky.
                    Murrary C. Kirk

The Journey of the Mayflower

In the early seventeenth century, a group of English religious dissenters, called the Scrooby congregation, immigrated to Holland seeking a place to worship freely. Ten years after their arrival in Leyden, Netherlands, a fear of losing their religious freedom grew over the dissolving of a truce between the Netherlands and Spain. This prompted the famous voyage which brought the Pilgrims to America.

Various agreements authorizing settlement and assurance of free worship were made with the Virginia Company of London, while principal funding was obtained through a group of London merchants. A ship called the *Speedwell* carried the Pilgrims to southern England, where they joined their chartered ship, the *Mayflower*. The *Speedwell* was to accompany the *Mayflower*, but a succession of leaks caused her to remain in England. The *Mayflower* then set out alone for the northern coasts of Virginia on September 6, 1620, with nearly one hundred men, women, and children aboard.

The twelve-year-old *Mayflower*, under the direction of Captain Christopher Jones, was known as a "sweet ship," meaning that her previous wine cargoes left a scent which somewhat detracted from the unpleasant atmosphere. Ninety feet in length, with a beam of twenty-six, she was capable of carrying 180 tons.

Thanks to William Bradford, principal leader and historian for the Pilgrims, we have some record of the journey. A general state of discomfort as a result of overcrowding, dampness, and cold prevailed throughout the trip, hampered by storms and strong winds. After two months on the open sea, land was sighted; however, it was to be another month before the small crew aboard a shallop would land and explore the new land. The voyage had been a good one in spite of the season, and the *Mayflower* anchored herself in what is now Provincetown Harbor, waiting for a go-ahead from the shallop crew.

The actual significance of Plymouth Rock has been disputed, as to whether the first exploring party landed there, or whether it marked a beachhead, later developed into a wharf. Fronted by a little channel, the large stone provided the setting for a good wharf. The Rock was not mentioned, however, in Bradford's writings. It was identified as the landing place of the Pilgrims by Thomas Faunce, last Ruling Elder of the Plymouth Church; this knowledge forwarded from his father, who arrived in Plymouth via the ship *Anne* in 1623.

The Rock has been moved to various places in its history, but finally rests near its original place, somewhat protected from the action of the sea, yet lapped by the waves in its historic setting. As an important national symbol, Plymouth Rock commemorates the important voyage of our forefathers.

Linda Robinson

SAMPLERS

Humorists insist that when that fabulous ship, the Mayflower, landed on the American shores it must have carried a record-breaking cargo of unidentified stowaways to account for the millions who now claim direct descent from its passengers. Nothing, of course, is said of the baggage of these fictitious ancestors, but it seems certain that the twenty-four women on the official passenger list carried with them their sewing samplers and may even have passed the time on that dreary voyage improving their stitches.

The sampler of the colonial period, a narrow linen strip usually about seven inches wide and two or three feet long, was used by the owner to record her techniques in the cross-stitch, the drawn-work, faggot stitch, petit point, darn, and the other fancy stitches which she might later want to study before attempting their use in the decoration of linens and wearing apparel. The sampler, literally "a sample of stitches," was no new thing even at that time, its origin dating back to the time of Chaucer, when they were known as ensemplers. One of the earliest historical mentions of a sampler appears in the account book of Elizabeth of York, which shows that on July 10, 1502, the following transaction was made, "for an elne of lynnyn cloth for a sampler for the Queen viii d. To Thomas Fische." Other early documents record royal inventories listing samplers as prized possessions.

The earliest existing sampler produced in America was made by Loara Standish, the daughter of the bold but bashful Captain Myles Standish, military leader of the new colony at Plymouth. On her long linen strip Loara sewed wide bands of geometrical and floral designs with home-dyed thread using eyelet, satin, buttonhole, chain, outline, and cross-stitches. At the bottom of her sampler she inscribed, with yellow and blue thread, "Loara Standish is my name" and below this, being a pious Pilgrim girl, she further stitched:

> Lord Guide my heart that I may do Thy will
> And fill my heart with such convenient skill
> As will conduce to Virtue void of Shame
> And I will give the Glory to Thy Name.

The first American sampler is typical of the period, being the product of a mature needlewoman, and its inscriptions and devices were to be models for many more to follow.

Samplers grew out of the need each woman felt for a reference work for the multitude of fancy stitches which she might wish to use in her sewing. There were few, if any, books available to these

women though there is an obscure reference to a sewing book printed by Peter Quentel in 1527 and later there appeared "The Needles Excellency. A New Booke wherein are Divers admirable workes wrought with the needle newly invented and cut in Copper for the pleasure and profit of the industrious. Printed for James Boler and are to be sold at the Syne of the Marigold in Paules Churchyard. 1632." The women created their own compendia of stitches by using them in decorative bands sewn onto the narrow-loomed cloth of their day. Later when they wished to embroider their linens or some bit of finery they could find the desired stitch on the sampler and recall how it was made.

With the beginning of the eighteenth century came changes in the production of samplers. The improved looms of the time turned out a much wider cloth and the samplers changed from long narrow strips to wider, more nearly square, pieces. The change in shape brought with it a change in design element. Borders took the place of the bands and greater unity was achieved in the decorative effect. Another change of this period was the change in age of the makers of the pieces. Before this time mature women had produced the sampler, but now they became the work of young girls, the showpiece which the girl produced to demonstrate her proficiency with the needle.

The young girls in school learned their needlework along with their alphabet. The girls ranged in age from little Polly Fuller who, at four years old, produced a sampler with two alphabets, her name, and the date, to girls in their teens doing much more elaborate work. Mary Smith, who was just five, turned out a very workmanlike job with the usual two alphabets and the inscription, "Mary Smith is my name and with my nedel I wroght the same." She became a bit confused, however, when she came to the date for she has carefully stitched it as being 17014. The older girls showed greater proficiency with their needles and usually embellished their work more elaborately with needlework pictures and verse. Occasionally the school influence became overwhelmingly apparent when a sampler with the usual alphabets is decorated by stitching on the multiplication tables. Another pedantic theme that was occasionally used was the map of the state in which the sampler was made. One such map-sampler, made by Elizabeth Ann Goldin in 1829, gives, in addition to the map of the State of New York, the population of the state, the length and breadth of Long Island, and a brief reference to two victories of the Americans over the British.

These great-great-grandmothers of our bobby-soxers left little record of any of the giddiness that we generally associate with their descendants. It is impossible to imagine the lass of the Revolutionary period swooning over a recording but we do know that they sighed for love. Their sighs are sometimes recorded on their samplers in the form of love verse. One little girl worked onto her sampler, in language that the bobby-soxer would never use but with a sentiment she would understand,

> Oh let my name engraven stand
> Both on thy heart and on thy hand
> Seat me upon thine arm and wear
> That pledge of love forever there.

The needlework pictures, used to adorn the samplers, covered every conceivable subject from portraits, contemporary buildings, and pastoral scenes to Adam and Eve. The latter were usually modestly hidden behind enormous fig leaves and one prudish little girl even clothed this shame-free couple in Quaker costumes with Cain and Abel neatly stitched into knee breeches.

The verse that the girls chose ran heavily to piety and goodness in praise of parents, praise of beauty and nature, and verse mourning the loss of kinfolk. One lugubrious girl, Betsy Cook, dwelling on her own death, wrote, "This work in hand my friends may have, when I am dead and laid in grave." And, under a willow tree, depicted a tomb marked "Miss

B.C." In all this welter of goodness and piety one inscription stands out for its vigor and honesty. It reads, "Patty Polk did this and she hated every stitch she did in it. She loves to read much more."

During the last part of the eighteenth century and the first of the nineteenth the sampler makers began to include genealogical data on their work. Usually the names of the parents with their birth dates were recorded followed by the names and dates of all their children. The date of the death of any member of the family was stitched in later. Some samplers carry back to include the grandparents. Genealogists have found these samplers to be almost as useful as the old family Bible for tracing the family tree.

There are almost as many samplers associated with George Washington as there are beds in which he is alleged to have slept. Some of these were owned by families who entertained Washington and are said to have been admired by him. And what is more natural than that the great man visiting his friends should compliment the family on the excellence of the wife's needlework? Other Washington samplers carry verse celebrating his leadership and there are many that mourn his death, such as the one produced in 1804:

> Mourn Hapless Brethren Deeply Mourn
> The Source Of Every Joy Is Fled
> Our Father Dear The Friend Of Man
> The Godlike Washington Is Dead.

Since the Civil War the making of samplers has gradually died out though a few still appear now and then in the needlework section at the county fairs. Collectors, decorators, and museums have taken up the sampler and there is a fairly brisk trade in them. Some of these collectors specialize in particular kinds of samplers, such as the all-white samplers or those of a particular period. The prices paid for samplers are not, however, in the same class with rare books, old violins, or grand champion bulls, so if you should find an authentic old sampler in your attic do not expect it to pay off the mortgage; you will probably find that its greatest value is in your own home as a decoration.

In the sewing classes of our schools the modern girl studying Home Economics has available books, illustrations, and patterns as sewing aids. Usually she makes her own loose-leaf scrapbook in which she pastes cloth with trial stitches along with descriptions and drawings of her new stitches. She would probably not call this a sampler but it serves the same purpose as the early ensemplers of Chaucer's time, a place to record stitches for future reference.

R. J. McGinnis

The Mayflower
(December 21, 1620)
Erastus Wolcott Ellsworth

Down in the bleak December bay
 The ghostly vessel stands away;
Her spars and halyards white with ice,
 Under the dark December skies.
A hundred souls, in company,
 Have left the vessel pensively,
Have reached the frosty desert there,
 And touched it with the knees of prayer.
And now the day begins to dip,
 The night begins to lower
Over the bay, and over the ship
 Mayflower.

Neither the desert nor the sea
 Imposes rites: their prayers are free;
Danger and toil and wild imposes,
 And thorns must grow before the roses.
And who are these? and what distress
 The savage-acred wilderness
On mother, maid, and child may bring,
 Beseems them for a fearful thing;
For now the day begins to dip,
 The night begins to lower
Over the bay, and over the ship
 Mayflower.

But Carver leads (in heart and health
 A hero of the commonwealth)
The axes that the camp requires,
 To build the lodge, and heap the fires.
And Standish from his warlike store
 Arrays his men along the shore,
Distributes weapons resonant,
 And dons his harness militant;
For now the day begins to dip,
 The night begins to lower
Over the bay, and over the ship
 Mayflower;

And Rose, his wife, unlocks a chest—
 She sees a Book, in vellum dressed,
She drops a tear, and kisses the tome,
 Thinking of England and of home:
Might they the Pilgrims, there and then
 Ordained to do the work of men,
Have seen, in visions of the air,
 While pillowed on the breast of prayer
(When now the day began to dip,
 The night began to lower
Over the bay, and over the ship
 Mayflower),

The Canaan of their wilderness
 A boundless empire of success;
And seen the years of future nights
 Jewelled with myriad household lights;
And seen the honey fill the hive;
 And seen a thousand ships arrive;
And heard the wheels of travel go;
 It would have cheered a thought of woe,
When now the day began to dip,
 The night began to lower
Over the bay, and over the ship
 Mayflower.

Pilgrims:
Founders of a Proud Nation

Oh come, ye Pilgrims,
  Victims of religious strife;
Rich promises I send
  For your new life.
Ye will work, those who come,
  With sweated toil,
And many a loved one
  Will enrich my soil;

But wealth in character,
  Strength beyond measure,
And freedom, freedom
  And peace are my treasure.
Oh come, ye Pilgrims,
  Muster your courage,
And build on my land
  A proud nation's pledge.

In 1620, 102 English Puritans, commonly referred to as Pilgrims, received a patent from the Virginia Company of England to settle in Virginia. Separatists from the Established Church of England, these Pilgrims were enticed to a new land by the idea of religious freedom. On November 19, 1620, after nearly two months at sea, the longed-for cry of "Land!" finally came. Although the Pilgrims hoped to arrive near the settlement of Jamestown, Virginia, they were instead, far north, somewhere near what is now Provincetown, Massachusetts.

Their first official act was to elect John Carver as Governor and to sign the "Mayflower Compact," one of the great historical liberty documents and the "beginning of government of the people, by the people, and for the people."

One of the most outstanding of the Pilgrim Fathers was Captain Miles Standish. Acting as explorer, interpreter, magistrate, physician, engineer, and merchant, Standish led the first expeditions ashore and continued exploring until he came to what is now Plymouth Harbor. The *Mayflower* anchored at Plymouth Rock until the Pilgrims established themselves, then the ship returned to England.

After landing, the Pilgrims set about building the town of Plymouth, beginning with a common meetinghouse. They divided themselves into nineteen families and distributed the single men among the different households; each family would build its own home and farm the plot of land given to each of its members. The first house built had to be used as a hospital. Because of the hardships of the sea voyage, the harsh winter, and the lack of proper food, nearly half of the original number of Pilgrims succumbed the first winter. They were buried on Cole's Hill, where the Pilgrims sowed grain over the graves in order that the Indians might not attack them in the weakness of their diminished numbers.

The first encounter the Pilgrims had with the Indians was one of mutual distrust. It was only through the wisdom of Miles Standish that friendship with the Indians was sought, although the practical Standish also organized and drilled the men, built Fort Hill, and furnished it with five cannon. Samoset and Massasoit, both chiefs of their tribes, became friends with the Pilgrims, and taught them how to plant corn and fertilize the soil with fish.

That first autumn, the Pilgrims reaped a bountiful harvest and were able to fill their two common storehouses. These successful crops and the abundance of fish, deer, and wild turkey in the area, assured another year of survival. In friendship to the Indians and in gratitude to God, William Bradford, who was elected governor after the death of John Carver, proclaimed a grand feast of thanksgiving and invited the Indians.

There were still years of hardships, famine, epidemics, and harsh New England winters ahead for this hardy band, but they survived with hard labor and a strong religious faith. Learning to live in harmony with the Indians and carve a civilization out of the wilderness, the Pilgrims laid the foundation for a proud and strong nation.

Shari Style

America's First National Thanksgiving Day

A little girl in Ireland once wrote—
"God must listen to the prayers of Americans real close
Because He has given them so much to be thankful for . . . ."

Thanksgiving Day Was Born Old

Through it all . . . Thanksgiving Day has survived! Overcoming opposition from members of Congress, outright disapproval of an American president, changes in style and changes of date, Thanksgiving Day in America lives on. The tradition of Thanksgiving has curious origins.

While retaining religious significance, Thanksgiving Day is primarily a "harvest" celebration. The idea of devoting a day to giving thanks for a bountiful harvest cannot be attributed to the Pilgrims, although American folklore would have one believe our forefathers "dreamed up" the concept. Statements such as these enjoy wide acceptance, especially by Americans: "Thanksgiving Day is a peculiarly American feast" and "Of all the holidays observed in this country, there is none so distinctively American as Thanksgiving, a legacy of the Pilgrims, cherished because of the traditions attached to it," substantiating, one concludes, the theory that if something is repeated often enough, people will believe it.

The Chinese observed similar rites thousands of years ago. In China, the fifteenth day of the Eighth Moon is called the Moon Festival, which marks the end of the harvest season and is a joyous occasion in the Chinese year. Candies and cakes are baked in the shape of the moon, and music, feasts, and games highlight the day.

Thanksgiving can also be traced back to a number of ancient festivals, such as the Jewish Feast of Tabernacles which lasted eight days; or the Greek feast for Demeter, goddess of agriculture, which was a nine-day affair. The Romans conducted a similar festival honoring Ceres, their goddess of agriculture, and called it the Roman Cerealia. Both the Greek and Roman festivals featured "sacrifices" to their dieties, combining these ceremonies with music and feasting.

Even the Anglo-Saxons, following a traditional autumn feast of the Druids, held a "harvest home" celebration, the high point of the year in rural districts. After the last cartload of grain was brought in from the fields, reapers and other farm workers enjoyed a hearty supper— sometimes served in the barn. These festive occasions included "substantial viands," an abundance of strong ale, with the master and mistress presiding over the merrymaking.

Harvest festivals are still held all over the world; for hundreds of years, European countries developed special rituals to properly celebrate the harvest season. In Austria, November 15 is known as St. Leopold's Day, or "Goose Day." Goose dinners hail the beginning of the new wine season; people traveled to the Klosterneuburge Abbey (built in the twelfth century) to slide down the giant 12,000-gallon wine cask in an annual ritual of good luck. Feasting and drinking are hallmarks of the heralded Octoberfest held each year in Munich, Germany. Other countries, such as Czechoslovakia use the corn maiden as their harvest symbol.

But where did the American Tom Turkey get into the act? Many folks assume our famous American "turkey" sort of evolved from oversized chickens. Actually the turkey was originally a wild bird endemic to Mexico and Central America. Early Spanish explorers took the bird to Europe, where a few gobblers made their way to Turkey and gradually became domesticated. Many years later, possibly on a return trip with those same Spanish explorers, the large fowl found its way back to North America and, because of its debarkation point, was called a turkey. Thus, in addition to many other foreign influences on Thanksgiving Day as celebrated in America, even the venerable "guest of honor" has distinctly alien origins.

Concerning the American celebration of this time-honored day, we return to those harsh times when the Pilgrims first arrived. After the small band landed on the bleak shores of Plymouth, the Pilgrims suffered through a winter filled with sickness and hardship. Forty-seven of the 103 *Mayflower* passengers succumbed. With the advent of spring came new hope; for each family had a home, and a friendly Indian named Squanto, who had been taken to England where he learned the English language, brought the Pilgrims Indian corn. He taught them how to cultivate their crops, how to net fish, and other Indian methods of survival. That first spring settlers planted corn, barley, and peas. They tended their fields anxiously as their lives depended on these newly planted crops. The corn and barley did well; the peas didn't make it.

After the long waiting was over and the harvest proved plentiful, it seemed appropriate to set a day aside for feasting and celebration. Governor William Bradford chose a date late in 1621 and issued the following proclamation on that occasion:

To All Ye Pilgrims

Inasmuch as the great Father has given us this year an abundant harvest of Indian corn, wheat, beans, squashes, and garden vegetables, and has made the forests to abound with game and the sea with fish and clams, and inasmuch as He has protected us from the ravages of the savages, has spared us from pestilence and disease, has granted us freedom to worship God according to the dictates of our own conscience; now, I, your magistrate, do proclaim that all ye Pilgrims, with your wives and little ones, do gather at ye meeting house, on ye hill, between the hours of 9 and 12 in the day time, on Thursday, November ye 29th of the year of our Lord one thousand six hundred and twenty-three, and the third year since ye Pilgrims landed on ye Pilgrim Rock, there to listen to ye pastor, and render thanksgiving to ye Almighty God for all His blessings.

William Bradford
Ye Governor of ye Colony

Hunters went out into the vast forests and fields and returned with turkeys, wood pigeons, partridges, geese, and ducks. Others brought in clams, eels, and other varieties of fish. The founding ladies busily prepared the foods, making Indian pudding, hoecake, and a host of other palate-pleasing viands.

Since the Pilgrims had negotiated a peace treaty with the Indians and their chief, Massasoit, they decided to share their hospitality with the natives and issued a "blanket" invitation. The Pilgrims were astounded when ninety braves responded to their invitation. However, as precursers to welcome guests the world over, these Indians did not embarrass their hosts. They had killed a half-dozen deer for the feast and introduced the settlers to the joys of oysters! The first Thanksgiving Day, instituted by official proclamation, turned out to be a memorable three-day affair.

It is interesting and heartwarming to note that from the day they landed and began exploring the countryside, the Pilgrims sought out Indians in a spirit of peace and fellowship. After a parley with Massasoit, they effected a treaty which remains a model of its kind. Each side agreed to refrain from harming the other and to support the other in case of hostile attack from any source. The Pilgrims never violated this treaty; it endured until Massasoit's death forty years later.

In later years, the governor of each territory in New England set dates for a "thanksgiving" observance. The Dutch people of New Amsterdam, later New York, began observing "Thank Days" in 1644. This custom of combining religious elements on Thanksgiving Day gradually spread from New England to other settlements. During the American Revolution, the Continental Congress established several "thanks-

giving days" for people to rejoice in victories won. In 1778, George Washington proclaimed a day to give thanks for treaties recently concluded with France. But Thanksgiving Day was strictly a New England holiday for 200 years, proclaimed annually by individual governors and, occasionally, by a President of like persuasion.

When President Washington proposed the first national Thanksgiving Day in 1779, Congress almost nullified the idea, claiming it was a "European custom" we had no business copying. Despite the ensuing turmoil, Washington proclaimed November 26, 1789, as the first national Thanksgiving Day. However, for the next six years, another national Thanksgiving Day was not scheduled.

President John Adams resurrected the idea in 1799, in spite of continuing opposition from Congress. Adams' version was slated for April, 1799, and had nothing to do with the original intent of celebrating harvests. Somehow, in the twenty years that had elapsed, the idea of thanks for a good and plentiful crop production had become lost.

President Thomas Jefferson almost dealt the holiday a mortal blow. He maintained that Thanksgiving was becoming objectionably religious and, as President, he would adhere to the proposition that church and state should be widely separated. Jefferson, therefore, refused to proclaim Thanksgiving Day during his entire administration. New Englanders responded by designating "state-proclaimed" celebrations. Jefferson's attitude was by no means a solitary protest. Abolishment of Thanksgiving Day as a national holiday was in force the next sixty years, as President after President followed Jeffersonian Democracy to the letter.

Our modern observation owes its beginnings to a persistent woman, Sara Josepha Hale who, incidentally, wrote, "Mary Had a Little Lamb." Miss Hale, however, was not a lamb when it came to the subject of America celebrating a national day of Thanksgiving. In every reference book or article on Thanksgiving in this country, Sara Hale is credited as "the greatest single influence in establishing the day as a national legal holiday." As editor of Godey's *Lady's Book*, a popular women's magazine of that era, Sara Hale wrote impassioned articles, editorials, letters, and appeals imploring the President to act on behalf of a national Thanksgiving Day. In 1863, her appeals finally caught the attention of President Abraham Lincoln. During a year bloodied by the battles of Gettysburg and Vicksburg, Lincoln issued his first Thanksgiving Day proclamation to hold the holiday on the last Thursday in November.

Even so, Thanksgiving Day's march toward national acceptance was hindered and delayed by the potholes of national discontent. In 1939, President Franklin D. Roosevelt, at the request of businessmen for more shopping time between Thanksgiving and Christmas, proclaimed the third Thursday in November as the national holiday. Despite the fact that the date had been shifted during the previous 200 years, Roosevelt's action evoked loud protests throughout the country, and twenty-three states refused to abide by the new date. Texas and Colorado held two Thanksgiving Days, to avoid offending either side. Political opponents of the administration reveled in the controversy, publically pondering whether the nation was going to celebrate "Roosevelt's Thanksgiving" or the "real one." After three years of confusion and protest, President Roosevelt agreed to return Thanksgiving to the previous date. Congress then passed a resolution legalizing the fourth Thursday in November as national Thanksgiving Day.

Nothing worthwhile comes easy; a day presumably set aside to thank the Lord for blessings received has been fraught with turmoil. As heads are bowed around the table this Thanksgiving Day, memories of tumultuous years past will dim; for through it all, Thanksgiving Day has survived. God willing, some form of giving thanks will forever remain a part of our national heritage.

Gale Brennan

Autumn brings treasures
  Of heart and of hand,
God-given gifts
  For the service of man.

Beautiful color
  Enriches the scene.
Red leaves and gold
  Now jewel the green.

Skies are much bluer—
  There's a nip in the air.
Geese travel south
  Where winters are fair.

Signs of the harvest
  Appear in the field.
Crops overflow—
  A bountiful yield!

Food for the table,
  Beauty to share,
Autumn's in splendor . . .
  God's everywhere!

Aron Christopher

The horn of plenty overflows
  with what the harvest yields,
As fruits and grain are gathered in
  from orchards and from fields.

Bright yellow corn and nuts of brown
  and apples ruby red,
Lie side by side with purple grapes
  and golden pumpkin heads.

Virginia Blanck Moore

House Blessing

Bless the four corners of this house,
   And be the lintel blest;
And bless the hearth and bless the board
   And bless each place of rest;
And bless the door that opens wide
   To stranger as to kin;
And bless each crystal windowpane
   That lets the starlight in;
And bless the rooftree overhead
   And every sturdy wall.
The peace of man, the peace of God,
   The peace of Love on all!

                  Arthur Guiterman

Harvesttime

The golden sun of autumn fades
  Beyond the crimson west
And waning, casts a twilight glow
  O'er a tranquil world at rest.

The chill of Indian summer tints
  The leaves with red and gold,
While Nature's paintbrush still awaits
  New wonders to unfold.

Over lawns with gay design
  A Persian rug is spread,
As leaves come whirling to the ground,
  Yellow, gold, and red.

A glowing bonfire, blazing low,
  Is dimmed with dew of night.
Wood-scented fragrance fills the air
  As embers fade from sight.

Autumn's scepter reigns supreme,
  Her crowning beauty near;
Crimson sunset, leaves of gold,
  The harvesttime of year.

                    Harriet Leila Rourke

Merry Autumn Days

We hail the merry autumn days
  When leaves are turning red,
Because they're far more beautiful
  Than anyone has said;
We hail the merry harvesttime,
  The gayest of the year;
The time of rich and bounteous crops,
  Rejoicing and good cheer.

Charles Dickens

November Shadows

With the final falling of the colorful leaves of October's festival, November's shadows appear. One by one the leaves of tinted gold, of crimson, magenta, shaded purples, and dying browns fall from maples, oaks, gums, birches, sassafras, dogwood, and sumac.

A note of regret and melancholy enters the heart at the first faint evidence that summer is over, that autumn is rapidly on its way, and that winter's voice is about to be heard. 'Tis then that the shadows of November whisper their final vows to the dying year. Regrets, yes— but still a voice of promise! The seasons come and go, yet they melt so noiselessly, one into the other, that our thoughts are always kept forward— to a reenacting of each one, beginning with the budding and flowering of springtime.

These present shadows of November are significant in their silence. There is beauty to them all. The stripped trees and shrubs stand sturdily in their rootage. The colder rays of the sun bathe them as in all seasons. Life goes on. There is a note of permanence in all the moves of nature. She is mindful of man, and of all his interests, all his dreams, and of all his loves.

All nature is the companion of man— in her realm are scattered all the hopes, necessities, dreams, and aspirations of his heart. And outside his own human realm are those who live among all these gifts that nature has so abundantly given as a free gift to all. There is a kinship between man and every inhabitant of nature.

As these November shadows appear, both bird and beast prepare for their winter days ahead. They have no calendar to tell them of the advancing days. They just know, for it was "planned that way!" And so, happily, they waste no time.

These shadows, as well, fall across the pathway of all who have lived their days of springtime, summer, and autumn. They fall gently, with an enriched hue— and also full of promises for the days ahead and beyond. There are compensations all along the pathway of life, the same as there are along the pathway of the year. God still stays in his heaven— ever watchful of his own.

George Matthew Adams

*Through the beauties of nature and
growing things
one sees the everlasting
presence of God.*

L. Leola Holland Damon

We Thank Thee

For the sun that gives us life by day,
For the moon and stars at night,
For the beauty of the autumn trees
That fills us with delight,
For the scenes about the countryside,
As far as eye can see,
For the warmth of a fireplace fire . . .
Our Father, we thank Thee!

George L. Ehrman

Thanksgiving Day

We think of Thanksgiving in harvesttime—
In the yielding, gathering golden time
When the sky is fringed with a hazy mist
And the blushing maples by frost lip kissed,
When the barns are full with the harvest cheer
And the crowning, thankful day draws near.

We think of Thanksgiving at resting time—
The circle completed is but a chime
In the song of life, in lives of men;
We harvest the toils of our years, and then
We wait at the gate of the King's highway
For the dawn of our soul's Thanksgiving Day.

Rose Hartwick Thorpe

Harvest
of Gratitude

Lo, the fields have ripened to the harvest, and the fruitful earth has fulfilled the promise of the spring. The laborer's work is done; he has planted, and he has gathered. Season follows season, each clothed in its own radiance. From bud to blossom, from flower to fruit, from seed to bud— the beauty of the earth unfolds. From the harvest of the soil let us garner a new harvest of the heart and mind— a harvest of the firm resolve to be the careful husbandmen of our best gifts and opportunities; a harvest of reverence for the wondrous power of life and work in things that grow, and in the soul of man; a harvest of gratitude for every good which we enjoy, and of the brotherhood for all who are sustained by earth's beauty.

Percival Chubb

Harvesttime

Busy days, happy days,
Harvesttime is here;
Corn is gathered, golden ripe,
While the sky is clear.

Hay is heaped in rounded mounds,
The wheat is stored in bins;
Yellow pumpkins, ripe to carve
In jack-o'-lantern grins.

The basement bins are piled high
With vegetables complete;
While on the shelves in bright array,
Are fruits and jellies sweet.

Nuts are stored away in kegs,
The popcorn hangs in rows;
A happy time is harvesttime,
Man gathers what he sows.

We send our thanks to God above
For glorious harvest days;
Who showers his blessings over all
In many happy ways.

Fairy Walker Lane

Thanksgiving Day in the Morning

What is the place you like the best
Thanksgiving Day in the morning?
The kitchen! With so many things to test,
And help to measure, and stir with zest,
And sniff and sample and all the rest—
Thanksgiving Day in the morning.

What are the colors you like the most
Thanksgiving Day in the morning?
The color of cranberries uppermost,
The pumpkin-yellow the pie tops boast,
The turkey-brown of a crispy roast—
Thanksgiving Day in the morning.

What are the sounds you think are gay
Thanksgiving Day in the morning?
The sizzly sounds on the roaster tray,
The gravy gurgling itself away,
The company sounds at the door—hooray!
Thanksgiving Day in the morning.

Aileen Fisher

THANKSGIVING
(Doris Lee, 1935-)
Collection of The Art Institute of Chicago

An A"maize"ingly Tasty Treat

What is white and fluffy, light, not stuffy (no, it's not a cloud), crunchy, often squeaky, and, in its undeveloped form, reminds one of a card game? Popcorn! This tasty treat titillates the tastebuds of millions of people around the world who agree that its delicious flavor is well worth crunching through the few "old maids" at the bottom of the bowl. For many years popcorn has been one of America's favorite snacks, but just where did this explosive treat originate?

Centuries before the first white man embarked upon a voyage to the New World, the natives of America had discovered the value of corn, or maize as they called it. An excellent source of food, it could be grown extensively, prepared in a variety of ways, and stored easily. As it rapidly became their primary source of food, the Indians developed several varieties, each adapted to certain environmental conditions. Throughout the Americas, each tribe grew the type best suited to its particular region. Nearly all of them, however, grew some popping corn, not only for food, but also for decoration and recreation. The little white "flowers" formed attractive garlands and corsages; and the kernels, when thrown into the fire, could, according to Indian legend, reveal the future.

When white men arrived, the Indians shared their secret of survival in the New World by introducing the colonists to corn. The establishment of the first permanent white settlement in the New World depended on this golden grain. If, in 1605, Captain John Smith and the other colonists at Jamestown had not traded with the Indians for corn, they could never have escaped famine and starvation. Likewise, the Pilgrims survived their first long, cold, harsh Massachusetts winter through the generosity of the Indians in sharing their stores of corn.

The Indians extended this generosity further by teaching the colonists how to plant, cultivate, and harvest corn. The new settlers learned how to fertilize their crops by burying a fish along with the kernels in each hill; and the natives showed them how to preserve the seeds of the most perfect ears for future planting. They also demonstrated the many ways in which corn could be prepared for eating and for feeding livestock.

Through this teaching and learning experience, a warm friendship developed between the colonists and the Indians. Gradually popcorn, introduced to the colonists at the first Thanksgiving meal, came to be a sign of peace and a token of goodwill between the two groups.

The tradition of growing popcorn for home use was continued by nearly every farmer throughout the next two centuries. Popcorn became commercialized when, in 1885, Charles Cretors of Chicago invented the first popping machine. Mounted on wheels and powered by steam, the machine could go anywhere and everywhere, and popcorn vendors made certain that they did. Poppers appeared on street corners, at political rallies, fairs, band concerts, circuses, and outdoor gatherings of all kinds. The taste-tempting aroma and fascinating action of the popping corn attracted people wherever the new machine went.

The improved flavor also contributed to the success of these machines. Whereas popcorn, prior to the 1880s, had been popped dry, Cretors developed the method of wet-popping in oil which enhanced the flavor. In addition to the successful sale of popcorn from the street wagons, the attention popcorn was receiving from Cretors' invention resulted in large-scale sales of popcorn on the cob for home use.

During the early 1900s, popcorn was given a tremendous boost by the film industry. As motion pictures increased in popularity, popcorn vendors selected new locations in front of the theaters. Very few theater owners allowed the sale of popcorn inside their establishments because their customers considered it too smelly, too messy, too noisy, and thus, too distracting. The vendors compromised by remaining just outside the theaters or setting up shops next door.

During the depression-ridden 1930s, theater attendance suffered a severe decrease. In an effort to bring business back, theater operators reluctantly conceded to the vendors, allowing them to set up concession stands (appropriately named) in their lobbies. Ironically, any theater not having a concession stand on its premises lost all its business to one that did. Apparently, the customers had changed their minds about the inconvenience of popcorn. The vendors, shrewd businessmen, placed their popcorn machines in areas customers had to pass in order to get to their seats. Theaters established intermissions so that the audience could buy refills. Consequently, popcorn began selling the movies; and a common saying reflects this attitude: "Find a good popcorn location and build a theater around it."

At the end of the 1940s, movie attendance—and popcorn sales—declined again. The newly invented television set was taking its toll on the film and popcorn industries. As theaters closed, discarded commercial poppers glutted the market. The leaders of the Popcorn Institute decided that the solution to their problem lay in the revival of a centuries-old custom— popping corn at home. To sell the idea, they launched an all-out campaign to persuade other companies to promote popcorn along with their products. For example, the Coca-Cola Company promoted popcorn as the best snack to serve with a Coke®. The Morton Salt Company advertised their product with this slogan: "Popcorn worth its salt is worth Morton's." Several breweries and salad oil companies followed suit and the Popcorn Institute achieved its desired result; the sale of unpopped corn climbed as television viewers enjoyed all the comforts of a movie theater right in their own homes. By 1952, the popcorn business reached a new peak.

Today, nearly everyone owns some sort of popper to make delicious popcorn at home, comparable to that sold in the theaters. Well, not quite comparable. A difference between home-popped corn and theater-popped corn still seems to exist. The secret is in the butter; theaters use anhydrous butter—butter that is almost completely without the curds and whey. Unlike regular butter, it melts at room temperature and, when poured over popcorn, does not cool and solidify. With the taste of this pure, unsalted creamery butter, the flavor of the popcorn and salt stand out.

Besides butter, color can also play a part in determining the difference between homemade and theater popcorn. The two types of popcorn differ according to color, size, and taste. Yellow kernels pop into large pieces of popcorn, white with an overall tinge of yellow. White kernels, on the other hand, pop into smaller, but more flavorful, pieces of popcorn. Since about 1935, theaters and other businesses have been serving yellow popcorn because of its large size and buttery appearance. For this reason, the amount of yellow popcorn grown in the United States is much greater than the amount of white grown. At home, however, many people still prefer the white popcorn.

Yellow or white, large or small, buttered or unbuttered, homemade or theater-made, popcorn is still the same treat the Indians enjoyed thousands of years ago. Although the technique of making it might be a bit more sophisticated than in the past, its simple goodness and delicious taste have remained the same and, in its unbuttered form, nutritious and nonfattening. A treat even more American than Mom's apple pie, popcorn is definitely here to stay.

Beverly Rae Wiersum

Thanksgiving at Old Sturbridge Village
Sturbridge, Massachusetts
Michael and Carolyn Manheim

Thanksgiving Day finds an extra bustling in the crisp November air at Old Sturbridge Village, as the preparation of a feast is added to the other activities of the season. It smells like Thanksgiving inside the Stephen Fitch House where cranberry sauce is being prepared, at the John Fenno House where a mincemeat pie is cooking, and at other locations throughout the village museum. An educational link with the past rides the air as easily as the aromas.

"But where's the turkey?" asks a puzzled young visitor to the General Salem Towne House. He had entered a kitchen filled with the fragrance of roasting turkey, but no bird is hanging over the blazing fire.

An interpreter shows him how to lift the lid of a tin bake oven, situated a foot or two in front of the fireplace. Inside the oven a turkey is browning, and the interpreter—a woman dressed in period clothing who looks as though she actually lives in the house—turns a spit to keep the roasting even.

"I couldn't go over to the general store and buy an oven," she explains to her visitors, "because they don't sell them. The tinsmith made this one for me."

And the blacksmith made the spit for the tinsmith, we learn, in a conversation that provides insight into the trade of the times.

Old Sturbridge Village is a recreated community of the 1790 to 1840 era, with approximately forty structures located on 200 acres of farmland surrounding the Quinebaug River in Sturbridge, Massachusetts. The Village opened in 1946 with the homes, shops, schoolhouse, tavern, meetinghouses, and other buildings of a typical New England agricultural community poised on the edge of America's Industrial Revolution.

Focal point of the living museum is the grassy Village Common ringed by a variety of buildings, including a towering Meetinghouse at one end and the imposing General Salem Towne Mansion at the other. The mansion was built in nearby Charlton, Massachusetts in 1796.

A horse-drawn "carryall" offers free rides to those who want to climb aboard its benches. One trip starts near the Common, below the Tavern, and goes through woodlands to the Moses Wilder Blacksmith Shop. Inside the granite building a blacksmith pumps his bellows to fan a fire and heat up some metal. Then he creates another necessity for daily life. He might have been hammering out nails yesterday, showing and telling how each nail was hand-formed from an iron rod. Today the blacksmith demonstrates the forging of spits for the bake ovens. Tomorrow he might be fashioning a new auger for the Pliny Freeman Farm, just a stroll away.

"That vinegar-y smell?" a farmhand replies to a question as he augers out holes in a fence post. "That's red oak. Want to take a turn?"

Each person eagerly twists the auger handle and just as quickly gives up this demanding chore, finding it harder than it looks. Task completed, the farmer goes off to split and stack rails that will eventually fit into the posts and supplement the existing Village fences.

From inside one of those fences comes the sound of gunfire. At closer inspection you can see farmers using antique flintlock firearms in a demonstration of a wild turkey shoot. To add to the aura, a plucked turkey, ready for dressing for the bake oven, is hanging from an adjacent tree. Inside the farmhouse the women are roasting other turkeys and creating a Thanksgiving dinner that includes stuffing, vegetables, puddings, and pies.

Around noon the farmhands troop in, fill up their plates, and go off to enjoy their feast. A welcome respite from the day's chores, this Thanksgiving dinner is practical reinforcement of the importance of the domestic arts of the era.

The historical domestic role of women, interpreted through demonstrations of daily housekeeping activities, extended far beyond the hot and hazardous fireplace cooking of the 1800s. Federalist women were skilled at preserving food by pickling, salting, drying, and other methods of stocking the cellar and garret of a home. They practiced "sick cookery," the preparation of homemade medicine. They engaged in textile production through spinning, dying, and weaving. And they did much more. But women were not yet aware of their own potential in the other crafts and trades, which were male occupations.

Everyone farmed, even the minister, the storekeeper, the lawyer, the doctor. But full-time farmers supplemented their agricultural incomes by learning trades and selling their products. A farmer with a feel for coopering might turn to this work when farming was less demanding, such as in the winter months, and turn out barrels to trade with his neighbors or with the storeowner.

Throughout the Village today, men are industriously splitting firewood. A team of oxen led by one of the farmers is hauling this wood in a cart, making the rounds of the homes and businesses around the Common and including a stop at the schoolhouse. It may be Thanksgiving Day, but the dead of winter is around the corner and the lives of the people are attuned to the seasons.

Late in the afternoon many people gather in the Village Meetinghouse which functioned as both the seat of town government and a place of worship. Visitors attend a nonsectarian vesper service in the glow of candles burning in chandeliers. The atmosphere of the services provides a fitting ending to Thanksgiving Day, as Old Sturbridge Village shares with visitors its visions of yesteryear.

Thanksgiving Mural

Create a mural
   With great expertise;
Paint scenes depicting
   Thanksgiving and peace.

Start with a mountain,
   Majestic and grand;
Drape it in mist
   Like the palm of a hand.

Sketch in the bear,
   The eagle, the deer;
Wind little streamlets,
   Icy and clear.

Plunge shaggy cliffs
   Straight down as they go
Or drop a worn path
   Toward the village below.

Show me a valley
   Bursting its seams;
Paint in the harvest;
   Lace it with streams.

Dapple with yellows;
   Touch it with red;
Rustle the wings of
   Wild geese overhead.

Find me a fence,
   Split-rails asunder;
Nestle the crops
   From chill winds and thunder.

Dig me a well;
   Construct a cool fountain;
Plant me some maples
   To color my mountain.

Place a stone seat
   By the mural, and then
Teach me to share
   God's blessings with men.

Alice Leedy Mason

Beauty Is God's Handwriting

Oh, the splendor of the Universe! For many, Thanksgiving time is the most glorious of all the year. God has dipped his paintbrush in his palette of colors and splashed the hills and woods and fields with robes of saffron, and crimson, and gold, and yellow, and brown, and scarlet. The maples and chestnuts and oaks vie with one another in thanksgiving beauty. The sumac dazzles the eye with brilliance. The sunsets are too gorgeous for human description. In this amazing garden of beauty, our lips involuntarily sing forth praises of thanksgiving, like unto the psalmist: "Bless the Lord, O my soul; And all that is within me, Bless His holy name."

Charles Kingsley

Country Thanksgiving

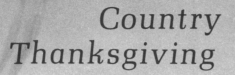

When autumn leaves have fallen
And chill winds start to blow,
There comes a celebration
That all of us do know.

A day for roasting turkey
And baking mincemeat pie;
A time for family gatherings
Neath cold November's sky.

A day to turn steps homeward;
A moment to stop and pray;
A time for saying thank you
For the blessings of each day.

A holiday to remember,
When time has passed us by;
Thanksgiving, a special feeling,
That memory will magnify.

Shirley Sallay

Off to the country for Thanksgiving,
To the old farmhouse, soft gray
Beneath the bare-branched maples
By the winding road's red clay.

Frost-rimmed hills stand nearby,
Woodsmoke embroiders the air;
And all is peace and love within,
With the family gathered there.

The table groans with steaming food,
And hearts lift to God in praise
For blessings that he has bestowed
On this and all other days.

Earle J. Grant

This Day

This day, I'll walk to some old shady elm,
Beneath its spreading branches I will lie
While scarlet leaves drift down around my head
And fleecy clouds sail in an azure sky.

This day, I'll walk beside a sparkling stream
That winds its way into the quiet wood
Reflecting in its depth a passing cloud—
On grassy banks find peace and quietude.

This day, I'll climb again on yonder hill
To walk through rustling leaves when trees are bare
To hear the sound of wild geese in their flight
When there's a tinge of autumn in the air.

This day, I'll see in all this beauty near
The peace and joy that nature seems to give,
The morning sun will find a thankful heart
That in this glory God will let me live.

Laura Hope Wood

A Day in Autumn

I waked and watched the autumn dawn.
   The blue twilight spreads swift and sure,
The sky lights up in splendor pale;
   The scented air is brisk and pure.

Now as the year draws swiftly in,
   The lingering shadows form a haze;
The silent garden's put to bed;
   We welcome lazy, restful days.

I like to watch the surface of the lake
   As wind-whipped waves go rippling by.
The sun puts diamonds here by day,
   Yet reflects the blue of sky.

A few brown leaves drift by the shore,
   Not sure of going anywhere.
The ducks dispute our right to stay
   And at the autumn sights to stare.

Thanksgiving comes around again;
   'Tis time to count our blessings all—
A time to think of all the good
   Abundant harvests in the fall.

We're thankful for our neighbors kind,
   For friends and especially family;
We're thankful for the freedoms here
   And golden opportunity.

The winds play music in the trees;
   The waves lap gently at the sand;
The deep moonlight shuts down the night,
   And gentle peace walks o'er the land.

Gertrude Bryson Holman

Autumn in the Garden

I walked down through the garden
This fine autumnal day
To see the autumn's flowers
Waiting there on display.

The chrysanthemums were blooming
In fullest beauty there
In rust and golden blossoms;
And on the crispy air

There was a hint of roses.
I looked a while and, lo!
A rose or two still lingered
As summer's overflow!

I walked down through the garden
This fine autumnal day
To see the last of summer
And autumn on display!

Georgia B. Adams

Thanksgiving,
A Family Celebration

When the children come for Thanksgiving, out comes the big roaster. Dinner is traditional, including fluffy turnips, cranberry sauce, giblet gravy, mashed potatoes. We do not, however, have the mince and apple pies. This is a sign of the times, for the children count calories and prefer to use them up on the main dinner. The small ones have dishes of ice cream while the adults have a fruit bowl, cheese, and crackers.

Toward evening, everyone is ready for cold turkey and thinly sliced dressing for sandwiches. It is self-service, for Mama is through for the day! Later we get out the corn popper and a bowl of apples, in case anyone is starving. We like corn popped in a rusty old popper from the early days, shaken back and forth over the embers in the fireplace. I use part oil and part butter and more salt than anyone would believe. My feeling is the oil spreads the butter more evenly—but this may be another of my notions.

It is a happy holiday and a reminder that we owe thanks to the forefathers who struggled in the alien land to find a foothold and establish a community. I do not think for a moment we had the right to displace the Indians—this is a black mark on our history and still is—nevertheless, the Pilgrims were refugees in a way, fleeing for religious liberty (but they imposed their religions on others afterward). History is nothing if not contradictory and confusing to me.

When Thanksgiving is over, Christmas is hard at hand—in fact I wish, at times, there could be just one more week between them. I have for years and years promised myself that I would plan so as to be fresh and rested when Christmas comes, but it seems I have just gotten the turkey soup frozen (how Don loves that soup "with things in it") when it is time to put up the tree.

I remember when turkey was a once-in-a-year dinner. It symbolized Thanksgiving. Ham was for Easter, along with eggs cooked in fancy ways. Roast beef and Yorkshire pudding meant Christmas in our house when I was growing up, or stuffed goose when Mama could get it.

Our turkey came to town from a farm near Black Creek, I believe, and I stood around waiting to see Father bring it in the house. Then that delicious smell of sage and onion and savory filled the house as Mama stuffed his majesty and tucked him in the gas oven (allowing plenty of time for the gas to die down around suppertime as it always did).

We were in Wisconsin and the relatives in New England, so a family gathering was out of the question, but Mama had a houseful, as usual—the family doctor and his wife, a couple of homesick students from the college, a couple of single members of the faculty. All the leaves were put in the big mahogany table and the great lace cloth laid on. Father always said a hurried gruff blessing, for it embarrassed him to talk publicly to God. He addressed Him in private rather as one equal to another, but at the dinner table he flushed and ran the words together.

Nowadays turkey is so available it is no longer a seasonal treat. At times I am sorry it is so common, for that first thrill of seeing it on Thanksgiving morning is gone. The grandchildren accept turkey as just another good meal. I won't go so far as to say it should be restricted to holidays, but a few things should still be rare treats, I think. Of course it always is a treat to me because, since I live alone, the only turkey I meet is when the children assemble for a week end or a holiday. One person, even with the help of an Irish and cockers, cannot undertake even a small turkey. The half-turkeys now available are fine for apartment dwellers but still too much for me.

Gladys Taber

Let Us Not Forget

We should observe this day with more than feasting.
It should be one of gratitude and prayer
To the Author of all good, a day of praising
For the blessings that surround us everywhere.
A voice sounds from the wilderness as clearly
As when the words were uttered long ago,
"We will set a day aside for our thanksgiving
To God for the increase of the seeds we sow.
"For His constant care that ever is about us;
For the promise of this new and untried land,
We will be grateful to Him for the mercies
That flow unhindered from His outflung hand."

Within our wilderness today, so should we
Be reverent and be mindful as were they
Who faced each threatening danger, meeting bravely
The hardships they encountered day by day.
No less than theirs, our future is uncertain.
Today of all days, facing paths untrod,
May we not fail in gratitude for blessings
That are bestowed upon us by our God.

Grace Noll Crowell

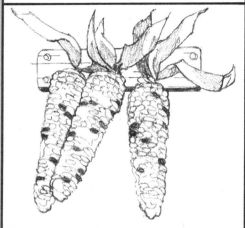

Autumn Days

Thy blessing, Lord, on these bright, autumn days
So filled with golden beauty at our door.
The fruitful earth gives of its generous bounty
In measure full, pressed down, and running o'er.

The apple trees with ripened fruit hang burdened;
The wheat field yields its sheaves of golden grain.
A lonely scarecrow watches from the cornfield
O'er mounds of corn and pumpkins in the lane.

Across the countryside and through the woodlands,
The maples have presented glorious fare.
The russet of the oak and golden aspen . . .
God's masterpiece produced in beauty rare.

Along the brook bright asters now are blooming;
The dusty roads are bright with goldenrod.
Upon the fence the wild grapes hang in clusters
And hidden silk escapes from milkweed pods.

The marigold now shows its wondrous splendor;
Wild ducks are resting on the quiet pond.
Chrysanthemums are ruling o'er the garden . . .
A beauteous summer rose blooms sadly on.

The woodland creatures now prepare for winter,
The squirrels hiding acorns all the day.
The honking geese move bravely on their journey
And tiny songbirds wend their weary way.

These brilliant days that lift our spirits skyward
Have filled our souls and taught our hearts to sing.
For as the earth rests from her fruitful labors,
We'll wait with her for the return of spring.

Marion Olson

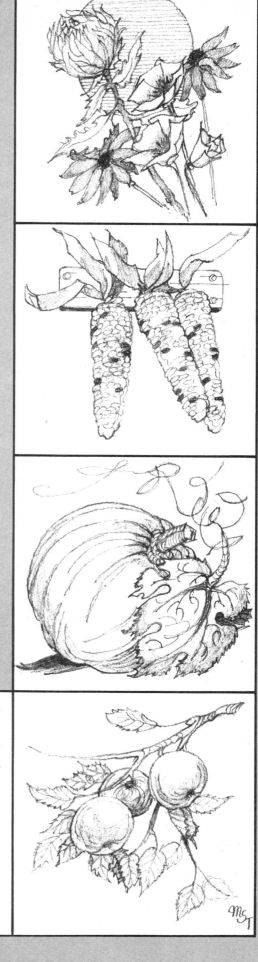

The First Snow-Fall

Selected from "The First Snow-Fall"

The snow had begun in the gloaming,
 And busily all the night
Had been heaping field and highway
 With a silence deep and white.

Every pine and fir and hemlock
 Wore ermine too dear for an earl,
And the poorest twig on the elm tree
 Was ridged inch deep with pearl.

From sheds new-roofed with Carrara
 Came Chanticleer's muffled crow,
The stiff rails softened to swan's down,
 And still fluttered down the snow.

I stood and watched by the window
 The noiseless work of the sky,
And the sudden flurries of snowbirds,
 Like brown leaves whirling by.

James Russell Lowell

HOME TO THANKSGIVING

Painted for Currier and Ives
George Henry Durrie

The Joy of Homecoming
In Durrie's Thanksgiving Classic

"Home to Thanksgiving," the print produced by Currier & Ives more than a century ago, is probably the most popular nineteenth century picture of American life ever published by the famous New York lithographers. It presents a typical farm scene in old New England. An ox-drawn sledge stacked with logs stands in the barnyard and a small dog frolics nearby. At the front door of the farmhouse, the family welcomes a holiday guest arriving in a one-horse cutter. The home and farm buildings, as well as the haystack and hills in the background are blanketed in snow.

George Henry Durrie, who painted the Thanksgiving classic, was such an expert with snow scapes that he was known among his fellow artists as the "snowman." Durrie was born June 6, 1820, in New Haven, Connecticut, where his father was a member of the firm of Durrie & Peck, booksellers for many years. His mother, of Puritan stock, was a descendant of Governor William Bradford of Massachusetts.

Durrie studied with Nathaniel Joselyn, a widely known portrait painter, then launched into a career as a traveling portraitist in New Jersey, New York, and Virginia in addition to his native Connecticut.

While painting family portraits, the artist usually lived with the family. This pleasant arrangement brought the gentle, attractive man many friends—and, eventually, romance. While in Bethany, Connecticut, at a church choir rehearsal, he met Sarah Perkins, the lovely daughter of "Squire" Perkins. They were married in the autumn of 1841 when the bridegroom was twenty-one.

His wife accompanied him on a number of portrait assignments; those were happy days for the young couple, although the family purse was often rather slim. Durrie augmented their modest income with odd jobs, such as touching up portraits, varnishing, and even painting window shades.

Soon they settled in New Haven where Durrie announced his availability in a town newspaper, stating that "he would be pleased to wait upon those who may be desirous of obtaining faithful and correct likenesses." While he was painting tiny children, young folks and their elders, he was carefully observing the beauty of rural areas—particularly during the winter season. On long walks, he would often stop to study the details of a door, a tree, a farmyard, a stone wall. In his journal of January 1845, he noted that ice-covered trees glittering in the sun made a scene that was "almost enchanting." He was enthusiastic about the joy of sleighing along snowy winter roads. His love affair with winter was progressing! He exhibited his first two "snow pieces" at the New Haven Horticultural Society, then the painting, "The Sleighing Party" at the National Academy Exhibit in New York City.

His life in New Haven was one of simplicity, fulfillment, and happiness. He loved to work in the evening, surrounded by his wife and family, and wrote of one such evening, "All is peace, contentment and enjoyment." During leisure hours, Durrie devoted himself to churchgoing and music. He sang in the church choir and played both the violin and bass viol. But in line with his Puritan ancestry, he would never enter his studio on Sunday for fear he would pick up a paintbrush.

By 1854 he had produced so many winter scenes that he held a public sale of them in sizes suited to the parlor or drawing room, for "admirers of the fine arts." "It is needless to add" said an advertisement in the New Haven "Register," "that no collection of pictures is complete without one or more winter scenes."

About 1857 Durrie established contact with Currier & Ives whose prints were fast building a rich panorama of American life. Then he returned to New Haven, established a studio, and painted a succession of winter scenes. This was an exciting period for Durrie because he realized that he could bypass portraiture and concentrate on his beloved snow scapes. He was a fortunate man who had come into his own.

For the next six years, until his death in 1863, Durrie continued to lead a serene and busy life surrounded by an adoring family and a host of friends. Although ailing, he continued to paint during his last year. "Few men have passed away leaving a purer memory," said the New Haven "Daily Palladium."

Durrie's paintings, such as "The Farm Yard in Winter," "Getting Ice," "Selling Corn," "The Red Schoolhouse," "Boys Skating," and "Going to Church," romanticized farm activities during the long, rugged eastern winters. Many of his paintings are owned by private collectors, others by historical societies, libraries, and art galleries.

It may well be that the perennial popularity of Durrie's "Home to Thanksgiving" is connected to our nostalgic yearning for a simpler life. This painting captures—forever—the quiet simplicity of a holiday on an old New England farm.

Mary Carolyn McKee

Thanksgiving
ISSUE
ideals

On the following six pages
we are presenting a selection
from Thanksgiving Ideals 1949.

Thanksgiving

C. W. L. Day

I'm thankful for the blessings I have,
For all that God gives to me;
And I know by giving thanks for them,
Still greater things will be.

Just to look at the stars above,
When I'm walking in the night,
Makes me humble, thoughtful, and glad
For the truly great blessing of sight.

Think what I'd miss if I saw the birds,
Yet couldn't hear their song;
The more I think of all these things,
Why, there just isn't anything wrong.

Good health I have, and a will to win,
What more could anyone ask;
That's enough to make it easy
To do the most difficult task.

I'm thankful for loyal friends I have,
As I've traveled here and there;
That's one of my greatest blessings,
'Cause a real, true friend is rare.

I'm thankful for the home I knew,
For the fun I had when a lad;
And I'll never stop being grateful
For my precious Mother and Dad.

When I get to thinking things are all wrong,
When I fill up with fear and doubt,
I have only to think of the blessings I have,
And it puts all misgivings to rout.

No matter what happens as time goes on,
Even tho Heavens themselves may fall,
I'm thankful today that I can know
There's a kind loving God with us all.

Submitted by Mrs. T. W. Zieman
West Allis, Wisconsin.
Our sincere thanks to the author
whose address is unknown.

Tommy's Thanksgiving

Mrs Gleta Smith

I'm thankful for a lot of things;
I'm thankful I'm alive,
I'm thankful that I'm six years old,
Instead of only five.
I'm thankful for my tops and toys,
And for my kitty gray;
I'm thankful for the big outdoors
Where I can run and play.

I'm thankful for the things that grow—
The apples, aren't they good?
The corn where we played hide-and-seek,
As in a little wood.
I'm thankful for the pumpkins round,
Just like a golden ball,
And jack-o'lanterns big and queer,
They don't scare me at all.

I'm thankful for Thanksgiving Day—
For pies all in a row,
I'm thankful grandma made them sweet,
She knows I like them so.
I'm thankful for the turkey, too,
How brown it is and nice!
And I'd be very thankful, please!
For only one more slice.

At Grandma's

George Lee Franks

Table spread for company,
Cloth, and napkins, white—
Best dishes arrayed upon it,
O, what a sight.

Turkey on the platter,
With upstanding thighs—
Red cranberry jelly,
Brown pumpkin pies.

Bouquet of celery,
Baked potatoes, hot—
The savory aroma
From yonder coffee pot.

Beans from the oven,
Butter, yellow and sweet,
Cream from the milkhouse,
And sliced cold meat.

Life preserver doughnuts,
Preserves, fruit and cake,
O, one is excusable
If he gets the stomach ache.

Sundry other dainties,
Life, it's worth the living—
Today we are at Grandma's—
Occasion, 'tis Thanksgiving.

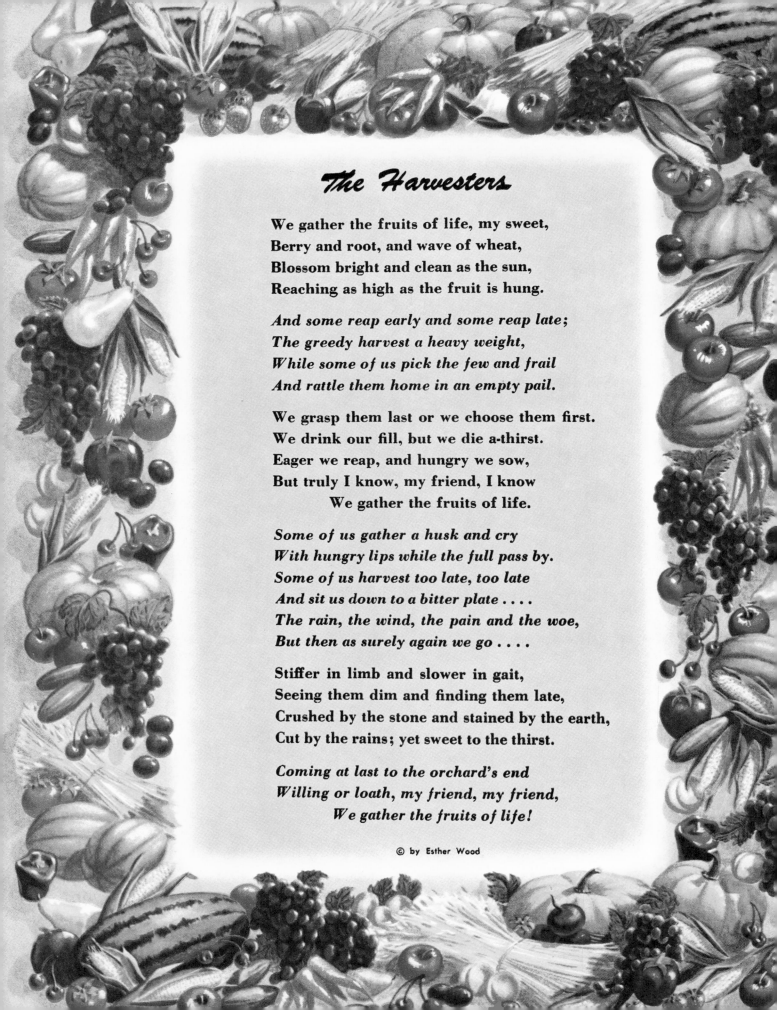

The Harvesters

We gather the fruits of life, my sweet,
Berry and root, and wave of wheat,
Blossom bright and clean as the sun,
Reaching as high as the fruit is hung.

And some reap early and some reap late;
The greedy harvest a heavy weight,
While some of us pick the few and frail
And rattle them home in an empty pail.

We grasp them last or we choose them first.
We drink our fill, but we die a-thirst.
Eager we reap, and hungry we sow,
But truly I know, my friend, I know
       We gather the fruits of life.

Some of us gather a husk and cry
With hungry lips while the full pass by.
Some of us harvest too late, too late
And sit us down to a bitter plate . . . .
The rain, the wind, the pain and the woe,
But then as surely again we go . . . .

Stiffer in limb and slower in gait,
Seeing them dim and finding them late,
Crushed by the stone and stained by the earth,
Cut by the rains; yet sweet to the thirst.

Coming at last to the orchard's end
Willing or loath, my friend, my friend,
       We gather the fruits of life!

November

Esther Wood

There was laughter and there was song
Out in the orchard yesterday.
Nature was dressed in gypsy garb,
Gaily singing her roundelay.
Out where the wild-goose called his mate
Winging off to the western sea,
Scarlet and gold and heliotrope,
Met in a haze of ecstasy.

Wee-folk under the harvest moon
Danced to the tune of the whip-poor-will,
Drank from cups of the columbine,
Sang with mirth while the world was still.
So as they revelled the night away
Under the starry-sprinkled skies,
Nature called to her prodigals,
Bid them off 'ere the sun should rise.

Gone are laughter and song today,
Gone are the merry elf and sprite,
Nature is dressed in somber hue,
Pale is the moon as it gleams tonight.
From the fields where the harvest lay,
Down through the valleys now at rest,
Nature, closing her weary eyes,
Whispers a prayer of thankfulness.

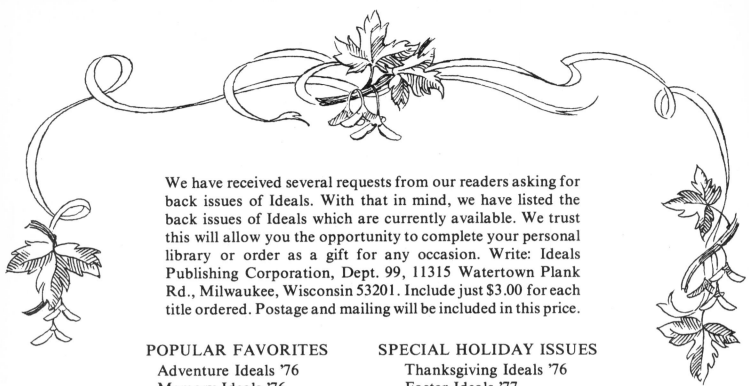

We have received several requests from our readers asking for back issues of Ideals. With that in mind, we have listed the back issues of Ideals which are currently available. We trust this will allow you the opportunity to complete your personal library or order as a gift for any occasion. Write: Ideals Publishing Corporation, Dept. 99, 11315 Watertown Plank Rd., Milwaukee, Wisconsin 53201. Include just $3.00 for each title ordered. Postage and mailing will be included in this price.

POPULAR FAVORITES
Adventure Ideals '76
Memory Ideals '76
Inspiration Ideals '77
Happiness Ideals '77
Woodland Ideals '77
Autumn Time Ideals '77
Fireside Ideals '78
Neighborly Ideals '78
Countryside Ideals '78

SPECIAL HOLIDAY ISSUES
Thanksgiving Ideals '76
Easter Ideals '77
Christmas Ideals '77
Easter Ideals '78
Thanksgiving Ideals '78
Christmas Ideals '78
Easter Ideals '79

ACKNOWLEDGMENTS
NOVEMBER SHADOWS by George Matthew Adams. Copyrighted. Used by permission of The Washington Star Syndicate, Inc. THANKSGIVING DAY IN THE MORNING by Aileen Fisher. Copyrighted. Used by permission of the author. HOUSE BLESSING by Arthur Guiterman. From the book DEATH AND GENERAL PUTNAM AND 101 OTHER POEMS by Arthur Guiterman. Copyright 1935 by E. P. Dutton & Co., Inc. Renewal © 1963 by Mrs. Vida Lindo Guiterman. FOR FRUITED VINE by Murray C. Kirk. Copyrighted and used by permission of the National Thanksgiving Association. SAMPLERS by R.J. McGinnis. From THE GOOD OLD DAYS, edited and compiled by R.J. McGinnis, Copyright © 1960 by F and W Publishing Corporation.

CORRECTION
John Wayne Print
The Homespun issue of Ideals offered a limited edition portrait of John Wayne in a 9" x 15" size. The *correct* dimensions of the portrait are *19" x 15"*. To obtain a numbered limited edition portrait, signed by the artist, mail check or money order for $12.50 plus $2.00 postage & handling to: Ron Adair, 13777 N. Central Expy., Suite 521, Dallas, Texas, 75243. Ideals regrets any inconvenience this unintentional error may have caused.

COLOR ART AND PHOTO CREDITS:
(in order of appearance)

Cover #1, Fred Sieb; Cover #2, Fred Sieb; In praise of the Lord, Gerald Koser; Autumn reflections, Fred Sieb; Mt. Washington Valley, New Hampshire, Fred Sieb; THE EMBARKATION OF THE PILGRIM FATHERS AT PLYMOUTH, ENGLAND 1620, by C. M. Padory, Three Lions, Inc.; THE MAYFLOWER, Fred Sieb; THE FIRST THANKSGIVING 1621, by J. G. L. Farris (American 1863-1930), Three Lions, Inc.; Thanksgiving dinner, Gerald Koser; Intervale, New Hampshire, Fred Sieb; The patterns of autumn, Alpha Photo Inc.; Autumn leaves, Fred Sieb; Autumn harvest, Alpha Photo Inc.; Fruits of the harvest, Freelance Photographers Guild; Basket of vegetables, Three Lions, Inc.; THANKSGIVING, by Doris Lee (1935-), The Art Institute of Chicago; Indian corn, Freelance Photographers Guild; Sturbridge Village, Massachusetts, Nova; Lake Michigamme, near Michigamme, Michigan, Ken Dequaine; Mt. Chocorua, New Hampshire, Fred Sieb; Chrysanthemums, Fred Sieb; Townsend Common, Vermont, Freelance Photographers Guild; Kaibab National Forest, Arizona, Josef Muench; Thanksgiving turkey painting, by George Hinke; Cover #3, Fred Sieb; Cover #4, Fred Sieb.